I CAN RIDE THAT THING

a collection of true, humorous farm stories

PAUL ADAMS

Publishing Coordinator – Sharon Kizziah-Holmes

Paperback-Press
an imprint of A & S Publishing
A & S Holmes, Inc.

ISBN -13: 978-1-951772-35-2

DEDICATION

This collection of short stories is dedicated to my wife and two sons. They are in so many of them. My sons now have children of their own and the stories continue. My wife and I have only been married for 53 years. Not long ago she told me, "Living with you hasn't always been easy, but it's never been dull." That was a compliment, I Think.

CONTENTS

INTRODUCTION

It appears to me as we become more comfortable with things like iPhones that we are losing some of the communication skills everyone used to have. I remember the time when men young and old would gather in a circle at a family gathering after a meal and listen to stories about people and places from the past. I have tried to rekindle some of that in this book and I hope the reader enjoys it. All these stories happened and added to the spice of my life.

EARLY YEARS

Most of our family vacations during the mid to late fifties involved leaving home about midnight, so we could cross the Mohave Desert and be up into the foothills of the Sierra Nevada mountains by mid-morning the next day to keep our car from overheating. Sometimes we went to the ocean but mostly we went to the mountains. There were three of us boys and there was always some sibling rivalry. One vacation we were camping at a state park and us three boys were getting our fishing poles out of the trunk. We had the gear out, and I don't remember what my oldest brother wanted, but he stuck his head in just as the middle brother slammed down the trunk lid. Back then there was metal in cars and even though it didn't hurt the trunk lid it didn't help my oldest brother's attitude at all. Dad came up to calm everyone down just as the oldest boy was telling the middle one to stick his head in there and he would show him the wonderful experience of getting your head slammed into a trunk.

A couple of days later Dad and my oldest brother got into an argument about where to fish because we had hardly caught anything. It ended with my brother grabbing his gear and announcing that he knew how to fish and would go find a much better place than we had fished so far. I think that he was about fifteen at the time and not able to drive. About three hours later our mom was starting to get worried. Dad told her everything was fine, there was still plenty of daylight left. My oldest brother surprised us all by walking back into camp with a stringer with about seven or eight nice rainbow trout on it.

We were all amazed but no one more than Dad. My brother proudly announced, "I told you I knew how to catch fish. I have found a great place." It didn't take us five minutes to gather up our gear and follow this proud young man to this place he had found. It was a nice-sized stream that fed into the main lake. We walked off the main road up along the stream and came upon a small yellow sign that read NO FISHING. Turns out it was a stream used by trout to go up and spawn. Kind of quietly my brother said, "I came in above here and never saw the sign." Looking from side to side my dad said, "I think we had better leave now."

Back at camp we finally had a good laugh, and I don't remember my brother and my dad having any more harsh words for the rest of the trip.

CAR TROUBLE?

——◦⁕◦——

L ooking back on my teenage years I didn't always behave like I should have. One summer I had a job at a gas station working from three in the afternoon until closing time at eleven P.M. Those ocean waves and warm breezes got to calling me, so I headed down to the beach. It was a beautiful day, great surf, just a little wind and pretty girls were everywhere. Well I got to having too much fun and lost track of time. I finally looked at my watch on my beach towel and I only had thirty minutes to make the seventy minute drive to work. I drove way too fast but made it to the station "only thirty five minutes late". I ran into the station buttoning up my station work shirt. To say my boss was mad would be a terrible understatement. He was livid. He was stomping mad, back and forth he would go yelling at the top of his lungs. Then he would stop and look at his watch.

Finally looking up he asked, "Where have you

been?"

I looked him right in the eye and lied. "I had car trouble."

That seemed to make it worse. Off he would go again yelling at the top of his lungs. He finally looked at his watch a final time and said, "I have to go to a parent-teacher conference right now otherwise I would fire you. If you ever pull a stunt like this again you are gone, do you understand?"

I quickly nodded yes. He left shaking his head and saying something about not being able to get good help. Since I hadn't had time to look in a mirror, I thought I should go into the bathroom and get cleaned up some before pumping gas. I was shocked when I saw my reflection. My hair was standing on end and my face and neck still had lots of beach sand all over it. He knew exactly where I had been. In closing, all I can say is thank God for those parent-teacher conferences. One saved my job that day!

THE DAY MY HUMBLE
FATHER BECAME A HERO

M y Dad was a quiet, humble man that read his Bible and did his best to live by its teachings. He didn't like quarrels and tried to be a peacemaker when he could. Dad was an equipment operator on a crew that put down blacktop on city streets. He would haul hot asphalt until it was time to roll it. Then he would run the roller and make the new street flat and smooth. One day while hauling the hot asphalt the man that ran the scales at the plant started in chewing him out about all the truck drivers making a mess with the used black oil.

The plant had a tank of used motor oil that the truck drivers would spray into their empty dump truck to help the hot asphalt slide out smooth and evenly. There was a low pressure pump attached to a hose and a wand with a trigger. There was ample hose to allow the drivers to walk all around and spray the complete bed of their truck. Evidently some of the drivers had just dropped the wand when they were done because Dad said there was a puddle of dirty black oil right under the rack where the hose was supposed to hang. Dad had always coiled the hose back up and put the wand on the hanger.

Human behavior is a funny thing. Some people just seem to take it on themselves to tell others how to live or act, or in this case, how to roll up a hose with a spray wand attached. He probably would have been alright if he hadn't called Dad and the other drivers a bad name. This guy wore starched brown khaki pants and shirts. He was going on and on as Dad sprayed his dump truck down. He finished by saying you "S O Bs" just drop the wand on the ground and now there is a puddle there and you have tracked it into my office."

I will never forget Dad telling me the rest of it. He said, "Since none of us seemed to be able to hang the hose up to suit him, I thought I would just hand him the hose and tell him he could hang it up any way that he would like."

It turned out there was one or two coils of hose left on the hanger so as Dad stepped up to him the hose came tight before Dad expected it. Dad was in the process of bringing the wand up to hand it to him when the hose came tight and Dad's fingers hit the trigger. Yep, my humble father sprayed the man from his shoestrings to his shirt collar before he could shut the sprayer off. Dad told me that after a moment or two it seemed a little late for words, so he just hung up the hose and went to get his truck loaded.

The guys on Dad's crew now felt that he was a hero and had taught the guy some manners. With a slight smile my father told me, "They all seemed to be enjoying it so much I really didn't want to take away their fun by telling them it was really an accident."

TITLE STORY

I CAN RIDE THAT THING

In the late seventies most farmers that ran cattle where we lived brought their cows home for the winter. If they rented pasture or had pastures far from the home place, they got them close to take care of them through the winter months. Running several head of cattle on a smaller piece of ground meant a large buildup of cow pies on the field. In the spring after grass was up and doing good people would then put the cows back out on pasture and let these fields grow for hay. To spread out the large manure buildup most everyone had a drag of some kind to pull through those soft thawed out cow pies.

We found just the right thing, a set of old metal bed springs. Yep, it would slice right through those cow patties and as the springs vibrated it would spread out the manure evenly and smooth. It was a little light, so we wired an old truck bumper on it to hold the front down. One early spring day my wife was with me while I was dragging those bed springs around our hay field. I started watching them closely in the rearview mirror.

After a minute or two she asked, "What are you looking at out the back window?"

I turned my head slowly and with a real flair I proudly announced, "I can ride that thing."

She didn't say anything at first, just looked back again and then gave me a serious look. "I'm serious," I said. "I'll get on the front and kind of lean into the turns. It will be kind of like a poor boy's Roman chariot ride."

She was mumbling something about a temporary loss of sanity or something, but I didn't care. This was going to be great. It had been a long winter and I could just picture myself riding those springs around in circles with my hair flying in the wind. Yep, this was one of my best ideas ever. I found some good used baler twine in the back of the pickup and tied it to the front corners of the springs as she told me all about the dangers of my idea. Mostly I just said, "Uh huh," and kept on tying the twine to the springs.

Looking up when I finished, I said, "Just go slow at first until I get the feel of it then we will go a little faster."

I hooked the tow chain back up to the springs and told her to go ahead. We took off slow and she was watching me closely. I had a little problem the first turn but after that everything fell right into place. I yelled for her to speed up and away we went. Man, this was great. I would lean into the turns and push with my feet and go skidding around the turns. I looked behind me and we even had a little rooster tail of green manure flying up behind me. I laughed out loud at that.

They say that into every life a little rain must fall and the rain that day took the form of a little high spot in that field that I had never noticed. I would like to think she didn't see it either because she pulled those bed springs right into it. Back then I only weighed about 185, but you see, when you are being pulled at eight or nine miles per hour many things come into play. Do you remember all those laws of motion they tried to teach us in high school? Well guess what? They are true. You take a human body traveling at nine miles an hour and bring the thing it is on to an abrupt stop and all that stuff about mass and motion and inertia take over and then the body continues forward in the air. Yes, I was instantly air born and flying towards ground that we had already spread. I hit face down and slid just a little on the spread manure.

I was green, but not with envy. My wife stopped the truck immediately and came back to me. Once she saw that I was alright she got a big laugh out of the whole thing. She thought it was funny but not funny enough to let me ride in the cab. She hauled me back to the house, in the back of the truck, to get cleaned up. Oh well, not everyone can say they have gone on a poor boy's Roman chariot ride.

PIG STORIES

SHE'S LIABLE TO KILL YOU BY ACCIDENT

———⟨⟨≫⟩⟩———

W^e ran hogs for several years before we started milking cows and selling milk. We used one humane ring put into the middle of the sow's snout to keep them from rooting and tearing up our pastures. Once we had three nice gilts that weighed about one seventy five that needed to be rung. We ran them across the alley in the barn and into a stall that was about ten by twelve and made from full two-inch oak two-by-six boards. The gate was also made from oak and real stout. I told my wife, "I'll grab them and get them over here and stick their heads out of the gate. You close the gate behind their ears and they will pull back, then you put the ring in their nose." All those great instructions just seemed to roll off my tongue.

"Oh yeah," I said handing her a piece of oak one by six, "If they try to run out the gate just tap them on the snout with this." Sometimes I guess I miss the obvious. We were both young and strong from farm work, but those gilts had at least sixty pounds on her. I then grabbed the first one I could and started dragging her over to the gate. I tried to force her head out the gate and it turned into a real scrap.

What I finally got out of the gate was more than her head and I was trying to pull her back when POW! that oak one by six hit me right on my left knee. I guess the gilt was smarter than me and saw it coming and pulled her head away from that oak board being used as a club. At this point I had a hundred and seventy five pound hog dragging me in a circle because my left knee kind of refused to work after getting nailed. The gilt and I made it about three fourths of the way around then she slammed me into those oak two by six sides of the stall. I took all the impact on my right elbow that quit working.

So now I still had this gilt and was kind of heading for the gate again dragging one leg. We were almost there when I saw my wife's arm pull back again. Evidently the gilt saw it too because she started turning away from the gate with me hanging on saying, "Don't hit me again, please don't hit me again." After that I just turned the gilt loose.

The surprising thing was my wife was pretty calm and said, "I wasn't going to hit you. You told me to not let her out by hitting her on the snout."

I had a lot going through my mind standing there rubbing my elbow but mostly now I was watching that oak board in her hand kind of like the gilt. On hearing this story her father laughed until he cried, then wiping his eyes with a handkerchief he told me, "I don't think my daughter would ever hurt you on purpose but she's liable to kill you by accident," at which point he started laughing all over again.

WAITING IN LINE TO SELL FEEDER PIGS

S ome things that happen in a person's life are so unreal that we can close our eyes and visualize them years later. One such incident happened to my wife and me in the late 70's. During that time just about all small farmers in Southwest Missouri sold weaned pigs that were started on feed called feeder pigs. There were several auction barns around the state that had regularly scheduled auctions for them. One hot July morning we were waiting in line, like everyone else, about twenty rigs back from the unloading dock. We had a nice group of about twenty five pigs in our truck and were worried about them getting too hot before we were able to unload. People were throwing water up and over onto their pigs to keep them cool.

I looked in my side mirror and could see a man coming up talking to each rig waiting in line then running to the next one. I thought to myself, buddy everyone's pigs are hot, you can wait just like the rest of us. I thought I was ready. This guy comes up to my window and starts talking fast with a strong British accent. He is all excited and hard to understand but I am getting some of it. It seems that his truck broke down and he had to get these pigs to the sale, so he put them in his station wagon and brought them to the sale not expecting the line to be so long. His Pontiac wagon had glass windows in the back, and it was like a greenhouse in there and his pigs would never live very long in his car. I finally asked him "You have your pigs in a station wagon?"

"I'm afraid so," he said. "Everyone else has agreed to let me go ahead so far."

Shaking my head in disbelief I said, "Sure go ahead." He then went to each rig ahead of us all the way to the unloading dock then came running back by. I was watching to see his station wagon and soon here he came. What a sight, he was waving thanks to all of us while his white feeder pigs were playing tag inside that station wagon. Up and over the seats they would jump then look out the windows, some putting their pink noses up on the windows. Now I really don't expect to ever see a nice mint green Pontiac station wagon with a load of forty-pound feeder pigs playing tag in it again, but we sure did once.

ALMOST OUT OF THE HOG BUSINESS

W e went through one of the drastic price declines and all but depleted our sows. We only had one left to raise a litter so we could fatten up some pigs for ourselves and a few friends. While at an auction I bought a nondescript boar by the pound. I planned to only keep him a few weeks, get my sow bred, get a little gain on him and hopefully break even on the deal. Well everything seemed to work out. He bred that sow and gained some weight, so it was time to haul him to town. The best market was in Springfield, Missouri's third largest town.

We had a well broken in 1968 Chevy pickup with some worn out wood stock racks on it that were just a little loose. We made good time for over an hour then hit the stoplights of town. We never did figure out what was so interesting or exciting about town to that boar hog, but he decided that he wanted to see it. He used his snout to lift the stock racks and had his head out and was trying to climb out of the truck. My wife happened to look in her side mirror and saw this great big old hog's head coming up and out of our truck. "The boar is climbing out," she yelled!

I don't know if the person reading this has ever hauled livestock to town but let me tell you chasing a big boar hog down the streets of Springfield didn't appeal to me at all. "Hit him on the snout with something!" I yelled.

"What?" she yelled back.

"Here," I said handing her a pair of channel lock pliers about eight inches long. She gave me one of those looks, kind of like have you lost your mind, and then leaned out the window and gave the boar a good shot right on his nose. He sucked his head back and out from under the stock racks. Then my wife gave me a different look, kind of like did you see what I just did? She sat back down proud as punch at what she had done.

That did the trick for at least another block and a half then that boar tried to crawl out again.

"He's doing it again!" she yelled before turning and getting her knees up in the seat to nail him again. From that point on it wasn't a real nice ride for her leaning out that window yelling at that hog and tapping him on the nose with those channel locks. We made it to the stockyards and got him unloaded before he got out of the truck. I guess all is well that ends well, but I would like to add here that a person can always find new uses for a good pair of channel lock pliers.

COWS I HAVE KNOWN

RUNNER

M y wife and I remember Runner so well. Her great uncle had found a cheap little group of Hereford heifers when we were first starting to farm and bought them for us. We built a small corral and I bought a homemade head gate cheap at a farm auction. Just imagine my good fortune that no one else would bid on it. I believe I got it for $17.00. Being just a little conservative with my money I used some old rusty nails in those little holes in the top of those big lag screws that held the used head gate to the alley posts. It wasn't exactly a pleasure to work with but if you pulled the arm down really hard you usually caught the cow. Now Runner was a real treat to work with. Every time you came into the pasture her head came up high and away she went running somewhere, just anywhere as long as it was away from you. She would go single footing away kind of like a Mexican fighting bull.

One day after we got the group into the corral, we started vaccinating the heifers. To hear my wife tell it I guess I might have been talking a little loud, well maybe slightly yelling. Anyway about halfway through the group Runner came running down the alley. I knew I only had one shot, so I really slammed that used head gate closed and caught her good. What happened next is hard to forget because Runner brought her hind feet far forward and surged upward shearing off my good used rusty nails and ran off with my head gate still on her. There she went kind of crow hopping across the pasture with the head gate making kind of a clunk, ker clunk sound.

Since I had been a little hard to work with, my young wife got right in my face and asked, "Well Mr. Adams you seem to know all things, what are you going to do now?"

My voice seemed a little quiet when I answered and said, "I don't know. I really don't know."

Since all the other cattle had run out of the corral, she said something about always having housework and walked off towards the house. You just can't believe what a shock it is to have a cow run off with your head gate. I finally came around, got a rope, and gathered up some tools. Some bad things have a good side. Running around with that head gate kind of wore old Runner down. I caught up with her in some oak trees and got a rope on her. I started dismantling the head gate and she threw a big fit, so I just let her go until she wore down. Then I would start in again. I think it took about three sessions to finally get it off her. But you know sometimes things have a way of working out. The very next time we got the cows into the corral old Runner went to town and became some other farmer's joy to work with.

BLACK SHORT TAIL

In our area of Southwest Missouri most people who run cattle live with endophyte infected fescue. It is a fungus that affects fescue pastures in varying degrees. Some cows can tolerate it and others do not. Those that can't can have foot trouble, lose the tips of their ears in the winter or lose the very tip of their tail. Black Short Tail only had about two thirds of her tail and when she got spooked that stub would go up and away she would go. She only had one attribute— she would always raise a good calf. One year she lost her calf at birth and we decided to give her one.

We bought a Holstein bull calf and put the hide of her dead calf on it. We put them together and she started butting him around for all she was worth. We let her calm down and tried it a second time with the same result if not worse. Her udder was getting huge, so we decided to run her down the alley and milk out some milk for the calf and relieve a little pressure off that udder. She always was a rip snorter but that day in the chute she did everything. Trying to get her to calm down we let her pull her head out of the head gate but kept her in the chute. There was about five inches of snow on the ground so we both knelt in it, one on each side, and tried to get a little milk out of her udder.

She was being worse than hateful. Back and forth she would surge in the chute. When our behavior is bad sometimes things happen that serve us right. I lost my cool, yelled, "Hold still," and tried to hit her in the stomach with my fist. Well I missed her and hit that metal chute breaking a bone behind my little finger on my right hand. Let me tell you I wasn't mad anymore. Hurt, man oh man that hurt, and I was instantly ashamed of what I had done. There was one good side to all of this. My wife was on the other side and hadn't seen any of it. I started milking with my left hand until I would get cramps then pull just a few times with my right thumb and two fingers. Then I would lay that hurting right hand in the snow. Things were moving right along until she happened to bend down and look my way. By then my right hand had a swollen place on it about the size of a big lemon.

She saw it and yelled out, "What happened to your hand?" I was thinking fast but nothing was coming up. Then she yelled, "Did she kick you?"

Slowly I began to smile through the pain. "Yes she did," I said calmly.

My wife started in on a tirade of "I don't know why we keep the old rip. She is just awful to work with."

As solemnly as I could I said, "Yes she is" while still milking a little with my left hand. Black Short Tail finally took the calf and at weaning time was bred back so we kept her. Just about every time I would get aggravated at her the lump of calcium on my right hand would remind me of my actions. I didn't tell my wife the truth about that day in the snow until we were both old people and she couldn't hit me really hard.

STUBBY

The story about Stubby is going to be like her— short. I don't recall how we came to own her but more than likely I was somewhere at a sale and she was "too cheap to pass up". She was a gray Charolais cross cow that never weighed more than eight hundred pounds in her life. I guess making her way and raising a good calf while competing with cows that averaged close to eleven hundred gave her kind of an attitude. She wasn't mean just stubborn and obnoxious. When she came down the alley, she would just about do anything rather than put her head in the head gate.

One day we were working the cows and I didn't recognize her. I was trying to lift this cow's head with my knee and telling her to stand up and get up off her knees. My wife stepped forward and handed me a syringe laughing. "She is standing up, that's Stubby," she said.

Trying to keep just a little dignity, all I could

think to say was, "Oh."

IT'S REALLY NOT DANGEROUS

At one point we ended up with a group of Holstein steers that weighed around four hundred to four fifty. It was time to work them and we had upgraded to a box-type chute that was on clearance at the feed store. It was faded yellow and not real pretty. Since these steers were small, I thought it would be good to have one of my sons work the "new chute". He was trying but letting most of them get their heads pulled back before he would catch them. It appeared to me that he wasn't pulling down hard enough on the lever that caught their heads. I had been in the corral and alley pushing the steers up to him. I asked him what the problem was. He said that working the "new chute" you were out in the open when the steers came out and he thought they might run over him. He was maybe nine.

I told him, "It's really not dangerous," and for him to go back and push the steers to me and I would work the chute. Now this chute had several ways to work cattle but the big advantage to it was you could let cattle out three different ways. It had a side gate you could let them out or you could open the head gate all the way and let them walk through. The last way was to open a lever on the side of the head gate that would allow the whole gate to swing all the way open and let big cattle out the front. Sometimes it is truly amazing that the smallest detail can bring about a completely different result.

Now he had been having trouble catching the steers' heads, so I wanted to make sure I caught the next one through and show him it really wasn't a problem. Only thing was I forgot that the lever keeping the head gate from swinging wide open wasn't closed, locking it in place.

So here came a four hundred and fifty pound steer running down the alley and I was ready. I pulled down on the arm to catch his head and the whole gate swung open with the steer pushing hard on the other side. The arm I was pulling down swung forward and POW caught me right behind my right ear. I don't remember all of it but from what I was told I yelled out, "I'm all right," and made running hopping jumps then collapsed in a salt trough.

Evidently it was quite entertaining to my family because after they found out I was all right they began to laugh a little, then really let go and laughed for quite a while. I guess everything worked out because after that day I never had to argue with my son to get him to push cattle to the chute. He was glad to do it if he could stay away from the front of that chute.

OLD JERSEY

M y wife decided when our boys were small that we needed a family milk cow. She was very clear about getting a cow with long teats that was easy to milk. I had a good friend that had lived in the area a long time and seemed to know everybody. I asked him and, yep, he knew a guy that had a family cow for sale. We went over to this guy's place and when I saw her, I quietly told my friend I wanted that cow. It ended up a three way trade. The guy traded my buddy a hog for the cow with an extra hundred dollars, which I coughed up, then paid my buddy for his hog. When the smoke cleared, I brought home the daintiest, prettiest Jersey cow you ever saw.

My wife was happy as a lark until she bent down and looked at her udder. "Where are her teats" she asked?

I had been so impressed by how smooth and full her udder was I had forgotten to look. I bent way down and finally saw them, short little teats about as long as the first digit on a person's thumb. My wife was the only person that could milk her, and she had to use either two or three fingers. That is still not funny even to this day. Old Jersey turned out to be a real milk cow. She gave us more rich milk than we could use. My wife made lots of butter and even took raw milk to school and showed kids how to make butter. There was only one problem, Jersey was a snot.

She came in morning and night to be milked like clockwork and went right into her stall. We milked her just standing there not restrained in any way. You could wash her udder and put your head into her side for balance if you needed to but those were the only two places you touched Old Jersey. She had little black horns and if you touched her anywhere else, she would shake those horns at you and blow snot. Otherwise she never kicked or stomped or anything. She would give us over two gallons at a milking so with a little foam on top the milk bucket was almost full to the brim.

One day after milking her, my wife was walking away from her and evidently something or some part of her touched Old Jersey on the side. She turned her head towards my wife and shook her horns at her. Out of a natural reflex my wife brought the full bucket up between her and the cow. What happened next was truly unbelievable. Her little black horn on her right side caught the handle of the milk bucket and snatched it out of my wife's hand. Now Old Jersey had a full bucket of milk hanging on her right horn right next to her head and didn't like it at all.

She began to turn in circles bucking and bawling. I happened to be standing close by, so I let my wife out and closed the gate. Every time she would hit the ground milk would shoot straight up in the air. After bucking several circles most of the milk had shot out the bucket. It was then light enough for her to shake it off her head. With a final display of anger over the whole incident she kicked that bucket with a hind foot. We laughed and laughed at that cow bucking in circles, but she might have got the last laugh because we had to go to town and buy another bucket before we milked that evening.

DOLLY

We had several neighbors that milked cows and sold milk. We checked into it and decided it would really help our cash flow problems, so we sold our beef cows and the few hogs we had left and built a grade C milk barn in our existing old barn. A neighbor was going to sell their entire herd of milk cows and told us about some of their cows that milked very well but weren't the prettiest in the world. We bought several and started milking in Surge buckets and then dumping the milk in the refrigerated milk tank. This was the old method used for years using a wide black belt with a circular metal rod that held the bucket and teat cups under the cow. When the cow was done the unit was taken off and the bucket hauled into the tank room. There the milk was poured into the tank.

All the cows we bought from that neighbor had already been named and several had definite personalities. Dolly was one of them. She was just a sweetheart and tame as she could be. She just had one problem. She was light in her left front quarter. That means that part of her udder didn't produce near as much milk as the other three. If you left all the inflations on for the same time that teat would get sore. If it was real sore she would kick.

One morning I went out and got the cows up early as usual and my wife stayed home to get our boys off to school. I was about one third done when she came out and started right in feeding the bottle calves. I think she was in the tank room washing out the calf bottles when everything happened. I had left the Surge bucket on Dolly too long and I guess she was really sore because all I remember is, I bent down to take the teat cups off and then I hit the wall behind me and slid down into the gutter.

My face felt all tingly and numb and my mouth couldn't seem to get the words out right. I called louder something that sounded like "slarrinng". She opened the door that separated the parlor from the tank room and there I was laying on the floor in the gutter with milk all over the floor, feeling my face.

When she got to me, I asked "Ithh ma faithce cave inn?"

She said, "No honey, the cow kicked you on your shoulder, your face is fine.

To which I said, "Huh Uhh. The kow kick me in ma haad," because there still wasn't much working with my speech. She then told me to look down. There was a big black muddy cow print on my right shoulder. I looked back up at her and asked again, "My faith not kick in?"

"No honey, your face is fine," she said. It took us days to finally put it together. When I pulled that teat cup off Dolly's sore teat she really kicked. Somehow, she brought her foot forward then caught the Surge bucket behind her foot and kicking backwards slammed it into my head, then her foot took me square on my shoulder allowing me to fly like superman until I hit that wall. About a month later I told my wife I wanted to change Dolly's name.

"What to?" she asked.

"George," I said. "Like in George Foreman."

POLLY

olly was another milk cow that was as tame as a family dog. You could walk up to her, talk a little, then put her out in the pasture. Genetics and breeding are an interesting thing to me. You see Polly was a big Holstein cow in every way except one. She had a white face like a Hereford cow and the rest of her body was black. Our neighbors told us there hadn't been a Hereford bull on their farm for at least three generations of cows but she showed her heritage from way on back the line somewhere. She was also a big cow weighing in about sixteen hundred pounds.

Just about any kind of livestock can bring a little excitement into people's lives and Polly was no exception. We were raising about 30,000 chickens and milking our small herd of cows and running a hay crew all at one time when Polly really threw herself a fit one warm summer afternoon. I was out in the hay field with the crew about six o clock in the evening when my wife drove out to us in the field.

She can trace her heritage all the way back to Scotland and her ancestors were really at work that afternoon. She jumped out of the pickup and started yelling all about Polly and something about her being so big that she couldn't budge her and there was a calf involved somehow. The boys on the crew would look at her then me and grin. That kind of made it worse. I was doing my best to keep a straight face and just barely succeeding. Then my wife began to lose patience with me which really added to the boys' entertainment. I got my act together and got her calmed down enough to tell what happened.

We had moved Polly's new calf down by the house under a big elm tree and made it a small pen. It was much cooler there and caught any little breeze that came along. I guess a nice breeze took the scent of Polly's new calf up to her in the holding pen where my wife had all the rest of the cows getting ready to milk them. Polly then proceeded to tear the gate down, knock down our main gate by the house and get to her calf. My wife had gotten to her and pushed and tugged and did all she could, but Polly wasn't going anywhere. She had found her calf and she was going to stay with it. At one hundred and twenty pounds my wife didn't have much of a chance pushing Polly around and she was just a little mad about the whole thing.

I parked the hay truck and the boys in the shade and drove home with my wife who was now starting to come around. We got Polly's calf and took it to a stall in the barn and let her stay with it then gathered up the rest of the cows. They hadn't received their evening grain, so it wasn't all that hard getting them up. I got her started milking and went back to my crew and the hay truck. Late that night when she brought a meal up for all of us, she apologized but the boys said they thought it was great hearing me getting reamed out like that. Polly, being true to her nature, hadn't offered to butt or kick or anything. She just wasn't going to leave her baby. When a fire took our milk barn and we had to sell all the milk cows, we could only keep one for our needs and to raise an extra calf on. Yep you guessed it. Polly was our choice.

BOBBY THE CALF THIEF

Bobby was another tame Holstein cow. She was just a pleasure to own. She was so tame you could even push on her and she would try to go where you wanted her to go. She really only had one fault, she loved calves. Hers, other calves, she just loved them all and wanted them. She not only wanted them, she took them! We never had more than thirty head of milk cows, so we didn't need a large holding pen for them. Mornings after the boys were off to school my wife would usually look over who all was left to milk in the holding pen as she walked by.

Every so often she would ask, "Has Bobby been in yet?" I would look up quickly to hear her say, "She's not in the holding pen."

That is when I would know that we were two cows short. When you gather up cows in the dark before daylight it's easy to miss one if she is hiding somewhere. My wife would be grinning as she took

41

over milking and I would take the pickup out to find Bobby and the calf she had stolen away. It was always the same. Bobby would be down in some trees or brush urging the newborn calf to nurse her while the new mother would be off to one side calling softly for her calf to come to her. Bobby would have none of that. She had that baby and she wasn't about to give it up. She would butt the new mom and keep her away from Bobby's new child.

She was never a problem to people so I would walk up, grab up the calf in my arms, and walk back to the pickup and put the newborn about a third of the way into the truck bed. Then I would drive slowly back to the barn where I would put the new calf in a stall and wrestle with Bobby to get the mother in there with her. When she could no longer see the new baby, she would calm down quickly and go back to her old self. She wasn't bad. She just loved children, that's all.

FARM DOGS

A PUPPY SQUARE DANCE

When we started milking cows we weren't exactly living high on the hog. We were living on a shoestring looking for a way to earn more money and help our cash flow problems. We did have a problem as there wasn't hardly any cash to flow. I poured a concrete floor in our old wooden barn then put in used metal stanchions and wooden feed boxes. It wasn't fancy but should work. We then bought some milk cows and started milking. The cows seemed a little uncomfortable on the concrete and I finally figured out why. The slope really made the wash water run out well, but the cows were leaning uphill while in the barn being milked. The thing to do was pour a cap on the existing concrete floor that wasn't nearly as steep as my first pour.

I ordered the concrete with chloride in it to make it cure fast. We milked early the day it was coming and had everything set to pour the new cap. It was hot when we started and even hotter when we finished but we were young and in good shape from farm work. We finished the cap then used a broom on the surface to have good traction for the cows then went down to the house and sat in the shade. Our milk hauler came in and picked up two days of milk then parked his truck just outside our main gate and walked down to where we were in the shade.

He started out by saying, "Pretty hot today isn't it." Yes, we said it was sure hot. He then asked, "Did you guys pour a concrete cap on the slab in your milk parlor this morning?"

"Yes, we did," we said kind of grinning because we were still wet with sweat.

"Did you know that litter of Border collie puppies was having a square dance on your new slab?" he asked.

"No!" I yelled jumping up and running to the milk barn.

What I saw in the parlor is a little hard to describe. There were puppy tracks all over the slab and concrete splattered all over the walls. They had had quite a time of it in there chasing each other around and around. They weren't black and white anymore, just concrete gray. Their little shiny eyes were the only thing black on them. My wife and I gathered them up, locked them in a stall and went to work refinishing that concrete. I was worried that it wouldn't set up right, but it did, and everything worked out all right. After we finished on the concrete we started in on the puppies and washed off what we could.

It took over a month to be able to tell what color or breed those puppies were.

I JUST CALL HIM BILL

I have heard it said never brag on a child or a dog because they will make a liar out of you every time. We heard of a man that had a stock dog that he wanted to give away. I asked around and it was said that this man knew dogs, so we drove over to this guy's place. I kind of leaned back when I saw the dog because he was an adult kind of blue-and-black-colored dog.

"What kind of a dog is he?" I asked.

"Believe it or not he is half Border Collie, one fourth Australian Shepard and one fourth Blue Heeler," the man said.

"Well he ought to make a stock dog bred like that," I said.

"I don't know if he ever will or not. All I know is he will jump on anything you hiss him on to. When you say get him you had better be ready because he will go after anything you sic him on. One thing though, you can't tie him up. It just breaks his spirit.

As you can see, I keep him in that kennel. I don't know his history. I just know you can't tie him up."

"What's his name?" I asked.

"I just call him Bill," the man said.

My wife went over to him and he had already taken up with her. When she turned around and smiled at me, I knew we now owned a stock dog named Bill. He quickly learned the routine at our farm and would go out with me to bring the cows in. He was a little aggressive and I had to teach him not to bite until I told him to. He also turned out to be a great watch dog and really cared for our family and our cat of all things. He was never tied up and was scared to death to come in our back porch. We tried several times during the winter, but he simply would have no part of it. Lots of mornings after a snow I would step out the back door and call to him. A big mound of snow would raise up and Bill would shake out his coat and the cat would take off from sleeping with him or on him.

One hot week in August my Aunt Eula Mae came to visit from California. We had sold our milk cows by then and had some beef cattle. She wanted to see the farm and I wanted to show off my stock dog. I knew the cows would be up standing in the pond, so we took off, me showing her the boundaries of our place. We were starting to get close to the pond and Bill was looking up at me for instructions. I had already mentioned to her that I had a pretty good stock dog. I stopped the pickup and sat there for just a moment then said in a strong voice, "Get them out of there, Bill." He ran up to the pond bank and looked back at me, so I told him again, "Get them out of there, Bill."

He proceeded to chase his tail in a circle and bark. I told him again, and true to form, he chased his tail in a circle, barking the whole time, then stopped and looked at me for more instructions. He seemed to be happy and ready to chase his tail again. I said the only thing I could think of to my aunt, "Well he's usually a pretty good stock dog."

I know she left thinking that I had a different kind of dog. The strange thing is he never did that again. I took him up to the pond several times the next week and he ran them out every time. I guess whoever said that about children and dogs was right, either that or Bill wanted to put on a real show just for me and my aunt because he sure did that day.

JERRY LEE AND HIS GOATS

I don't remember why we decided to get in the goat business. We probably saw some sell high and decided to give them a try. We bought some of this and that, whatever was cheap and had some problems, so we sold our cheap stuff and started looking for a herd from a private party. We found an individual wanting to sell his herd in Northern Arkansas and drove down to look at his Boar cross goats. We made a deal to buy them all and then he asked if we wanted to buy the guard dog too. I asked him what he wanted for the dog and he said one hundred dollars. I looked at the adult Pyrenees dog and asked, "Is he any good?"

"He is the best dog we have ever had," the man said.

"Is he one hundred per cent Pyrenees?" I asked.

The man said that he didn't know, he just showed up on his place and took up with his goats. He then told us that the dog would even go down and keep coyotes from eating a dead cow that was across the fence on a neighbor's place. That sounded pretty good to me, so we bought him too and hauled him home in the stock trailer with the goats. We had no idea of how good he really was. On the way home my wife came up with the name of Jerry Lee.

We put Jerry Lee and his goats in a pen for four or five days to let them get settled down and used to us. I worked half days on Saturday, so I asked my wife to let Jerry Lee and the goats out of the small pen into the front pasture that morning. She told me what happened when I got home.

She said she opened the gate and walked off a ways to make sure they came out. The goats and Jerry came out and just milled around in front of the gate. Jerry walked all through them then left and ran the whole perimeter inside the fence of the front pasture, but the goats stayed where they were. She said he came trotting back up then walked all through the herd then led off. She couldn't believe it. He had made them stay there until he checked it out then came back and led his herd out after he had decided it was alright. They followed him like little children. We were just starting to learn about guard dogs.

Jerry's viewpoint was that the goats were his and he allowed us to feed him and be around them. He would growl and snap at the goats that tried to eat his food but with all that noise he never actually bit one. What he said was law to his goats. Once we saw him run towards the road barking at a stray dog. The young goats didn't run behind him like he wanted so he nipped them to make them get back.

Then he would position himself between the threat and his goats and tell the world what he would do if they got too close.

The intuitive abilities of these dogs are unreal. One time we decided that we needed to catch him to worm him or something. He liked my wife and allowed me to live on the farm. We came up with a plan to catch him in the pole barn. My wife put his dog food in a bowl right in front of the barn with the big wire gates open and he came up. She let him eat a little then walked forward and moved his bowl farther into the barn about two feet. It worked. He came up and started eating again. After a little bit she walked up and moved his bowl in farther. He looked from side to side at the open gates then backed up about three steps and sat down. We went through this for forty five minutes before we gave up, gave him all his feed and went to the house.

He would only come into the barn when we let the goats in during bad weather. We raised pups out of Jerry Lee and he taught them well but we never had one that could do what he could. We never knew how old he was, but time began to catch up with him. We found him one winter morning curled up in the pole barn. It seemed to be fitting for him to die in the barn guarding his herd, good dog that he was, Jerry Lee.

SOMETIMES GOATS MAKE LIFE VERY INTERESTING

A GOAT AND A SET OF
WOODEN STOCK RACKS

Some farmers in Southwest Missouri in the late seventies had metal stock racks while most of us on the lower end of the economic scale owned wooden ones that usually got a little loose after they were broken in. It was kind of handy because you could usually tell who was coming down the road from the sound of those worn out stock racks banging around on the truck.

One day while repairing a brace and corner post at the main gate to our back pasture my wife drove up to me in our pickup. We had only lived there less than two years. She had our one lone goat in the back of the truck with the wooden stock racks on. To say that she was just a little worked up is an understatement. She started right in all about "that blasted goat eating her flowers and shrubs and how he always gets loose and today he had busted through the screen and messed all over the back porch". She told me she had had it and she was going to haul him up to the cattle in the pasture and he could just stay up there and live with them!

Being very intelligent and well versed in conversation I knew exactly what to say. I nodded my head and did my best to look concerned but said nothing. Both of our young sons were in there and I doubt if they had ever seen their mother this worked up about anything. That goat had always been a problem. One night he got loose so I got to him and tied him up to some bush so I could get some sleep. The next morning it was obvious I had picked the wrong one because he had eaten my wife's lilac bush down to the ground. He got loose about a week after that, so I tied him up to the propane tank and he kept waking us up all night tapping his horns against the tank. So, it wasn't a huge surprise she had had all she could take from that goat.

She drove away with our two sons standing up on the floor of the cab looking kind of bug eyed. It was a beautiful clear early summer morning, so I continued working on my corner post. It was only about ten minutes later I began to hear the most awful racket. BANG BOOM, then a pause and it would go again. I stopped working and looked up as the sound was getting closer. It's not every day that a farmer looks up and sees his wife doing her best to run over a goat in his pasture. The goat thought it was a kind of new game and would jump and spring over to one side with my normally sane wife behind him in our truck doing her best to run him down. Then it dawned on me they were getting closer. The goat ran out the gate kicking up his heels, twisting his head and kind of spring jumping towards the house.

She skidded the truck to a stop halfway through the gate and yelled, "I tried everything I could to get him to stay up there. I would shoo him away and he would beat me back to the truck every time so now I'm going to run over him!"

I looked down at our boys who were holding on to the dash for all they were worth and kind of nodded one time. Then off she went again after the goat with those stock racks banging up and down on the truck, BANG BOOM BANG BANG.

I finished my work on the corner and walked down to the house. The goat was very much alive and eating some bush in the back yard. I eased up and looked through the torn screen into the back porch. She was there sweeping up all those goat pellets. She sensed I was there and said quite calmly, "I want you to shoot that goat today."

Maybe it was just my imagination, but she really seemed to be smiling when she fried up those goat chops later that week

A GOAT FOR EASTER

I have a good friend named John. We have been in a few business ventures together and had some fun along life's path. In the eighties we were both in our thirties and went trick or treating one Halloween night. We had costumes and masks on and went to several people's houses that we knew. We would knock and when the people came to the door these two grown men would say trick or treat and stand there waiting for candy. We even went to John's preacher's house. When the people found out who we were they would call over their friends and have them guess who we were. Back then there wasn't nearly as much meanness going on, so we never got close to being shot.

Time went along and I think John's kids were about eight and ten. I was at a livestock auction just before Easter and they ran in the cutest little black Nubian goat you ever saw. He was just about a week or two old with long floppy ears. I knew immediately what I was going to do. I bought that little fella and stopped by the feed store on the way home for a lamb nipple. Now we lived on a small farm in the country, but John lived in the nicest part of town in a beautiful home.

Before daylight Easter morning my youngest son and I crept up and tied that little goat to John's pickup door handle with a red ribbon around his neck holding the lamb nipple. I knew he wouldn't have a way to feed it. A nice note was attached reading Happy Easter. I did my best to stay away from his office until late that week and finally gave up and went in. I made up some lame excuse for being there.

My buddy John was more than just a little grumpy. I asked him what was wrong. He started in. "My kids came running in the house Easter morning with a baby goat somebody tied to my truck with a note on it saying Happy Easter." He said they called their friends and soon all the neighborhood kids were in his living room playing with that goat.

Weeks later he was getting worse because the goat was getting bigger and putting out more pellets. I guess the last straw was when John came home one day, and the goat walked up out of the living room to greet him. He convinced his kids that the goat would never be happy unless it ran and played with other goats. He ended up giving it to a lady that lived on the edge of town where the kids could go see it. He would bring it up every once in a while, and with a steely voice and looking right at me say, "I sure would like to find out who gave my kids that goat."

I would just do my best to look really dumb and say, "I just don't know."

Believe it or not we are still good friends.

FARM TRUCKS

THE DODGE

If the reader has never had the opportunity to ride in an old farm truck they have really missed out. It usually takes several years for one to reach the status of 'Farm Truck.' By then it has a good supply of empty vaccine bottles and various other half used stuff or the empty wrappers of them. We don't want to forget some tow chains on the floor and always an empty feed sack or two for absolute emergencies. There is usually an aerosol spray can of something on the dash to keep the feed store receipts from flying away when you open the door. We owned such a truck and called it "The Dodge."

We really needed a four-wheel-drive pickup. Our 1968 Chevy was all but shot. My young wife waited in the nice clean showroom while I test drove several lower priced trucks. She was doing her best to keep our two sons in line when she saw someone drive up in front of the showroom in an older ugly faded brown Dodge Power Wagon. She told me later when she saw it her only thought was, *I wonder who the poor soul is that bought that ugly thing?*

Much to her unpleasant surprise her husband climbed out of it and walked up to her with a huge smile. "Do you like it?" I asked.

"You bought that?" she asked.

I just knew she couldn't believe we now owned a tall Dodge Power Wagon. Then she turned her head and gave me a real faraway look and I knew she was just like me and almost too happy to contain herself. Well it turns out she didn't feel like me at all. She just hated that truck. It was a little hard to start and you had to really pump the gas pedal a lot while trying to get it started, but it almost always started before the battery ground down. That seemed to make her mad for some reason.

We have so many memories of that old truck, good ones for me, not so good ones for her. I could see her set her jaw and start to get mad every time she tried to start it. One day we were chasing a calf that needed some doctoring over some rough ground. I had been standing in the back calling out helpful hints like, "go faster go faster, we'll never catch him if you don't get closer." Just stuff like that. I leaned far out and started to throw a loop when she ran over a big rock. I hit the ground and rolled. She got it stopped with me slightly under the truck looking at the rough tread on the driver's rear tire. I crawled out and looked at her sitting there.

She had this strange look on her face like she had just missed an opportunity or something. I don't remember if we ever caught that calf, but I do remember that after I saw that look, I made sure I didn't fall out again.

I sure miss that old truck, she doesn't so much.

GEARS, NUTS AND BOLTS

I have a good friend that can fix anything. From lawn mowers to diesel engines, Donnie can repair them. I, on the other hand, have slightly less ability. Oh, I can change spark plugs, water pumps or alternators, stuff like that, but that's really about all. At one time we had a Pontiac Station Wagon with that vinyl stuff on the side that was supposed to look like wood. The transmission started to slip, so I told my wife that all it really needed was to have the fluid changed. She was washing dishes at the time. She turned and looked at me but didn't say anything. I thought that was a little odd as I drove off to the parts house.

I bought a kit that was supposed to have everything in it and came home. Man was I glad I opened that kit outside because it had all kinds of stuff in it. I knew I didn't need all of it but there still wasn't any reason for her to see all of it. I pulled the pan off and found the new gasket that went on it then looked up in there for the filter. You just can't believe everything there is in an automatic transmission when you pull the pan off. They look kind of like those space ships you see in movies. I looked back in the parts and found the new filter then looked around under there until I found it. I took it out and put the new one in. See? This wasn't all that hard. I put my new gasket on and tightened the pan back on all in about two hours. This was really going good. I filled it up with fluid and started it up.

It idled just fine, so I put it in gear. A strange thing happened, it died. I tried it several more times with the same result. I thought it through and decided that I need to raise the idle speed. I looked all around the carburetor and found that little screw and turned it up a couple of turns. When I started it up it ran away with itself, so I shut it down quickly. Then I tried to get it back to just a little faster than it was. After several tries, I felt I had it just right. I could put it in gear and it wouldn't die. I couldn't wait to show my young wife what I had done. I didn't even take time to get cleaned up, just wiped most of the grease off my hands.

"See?" I told her after I started it up. "It idles fine and doesn't die when you put it in gear," I said as I put it in gear. It was still a little faster idle than before and the car started moving forward. I managed to get my feet inside by the time it shifted into second gear. It was still gaining speed and heading for a fence when I finally got it shut down. I could hear her laughter all the way over to where I ended up by the fence. I turned the engine off and climbed out.

"You really have it fixed now," she yelled. "It can drive itself."

We traded that car with the transmission still slipping.

And now days everyone thinks that self-driving cars are new.

OLD HAY TRUCKS

W e had a commercial poultry operation and were milking cows at the same time, but always needed more hay, so I had one of my "better ideas". We would buy a flatbed hay truck and hire out to haul square bales from the field to the barn and use that money to buy hay. After all, hay hauling was mostly done in the late afternoon and night and we weren't working at night. It really meant just more labor at night. Good idea, huh?

I bought an early 1960's cab over GMC with a twenty-four-foot bed and went into business. The cab tilted over forward to work on the motor, so that meant the driver sat right on top of the motor which was under the floorboard. The floor had more than just a few holes in it, so all that engine heat drifted up into the cab. The truck had several holes in the exhaust pipes but with both windows open it seemed to me that those fumes would mostly flow right on through. Now everyone knows that farmers put up hay in the summer and when you added everything up it was kind of like driving inside a convection oven that had auto exhaust flowing up into it. I never could figure out what the big attraction was for wasps to build a new nest on that motor. My wife just reminded me to mention that there was usually a few of them coming up through the holes in the floor. It seemed to really set her on edge when she would drive that old truck. Probably the most disagreeable thing about the truck was the noise you had to contend with while driving it. With all those holes in the exhaust pipes you could barely hear yourself think.

Being a conservative person and always keeping an eye on expenses I usually had my wife drive quite a bit. We ran a crew of young farm boys and she spent many hot evenings and nights driving that truck and trying to hear me over the exhaust noise. Well it was bound to happen. One hot July afternoon we couldn't get any help and we were hauling in our own hay, just me and her. We had bought a hay loader by then and if she steered right and caught those bales right they would come right up the chain to me where I would stack them on the bed. We got into a small square end of the field where it was hard to turn and she ran over one bale then another. I yelled out that we were trying to load them into the truck not run over them.

A very strange thing happened. I heard the motor shut off and her door open. She slammed it shut and took off stomping for the house. I want to stop here and add that sometimes we hear words that seem exactly the right thing to say later. I don't know where I heard the phrase but I used it then.

Standing proudly with my fists on my waist I yelled out, "Hey, does this mean you quit?"

She spun around and glared at me. If looks could kill, well I think I'll stop here.

OTHER STUFF

ONE UGLY TURKEY

Sometimes inspirations kind of pop into my head. I never really know where they come from, they just appear. One fall after our sons were grown and gone, I got to wondering how big I could grow a turkey. I decided to see if I could get one to weigh fifty pounds. I had a friend that worked as a field representative for a turkey company overseeing the growing operations. I asked him if they lost a few turkeys during loading like we did when we were raising chickens. He said yes, there was usually one or two walking around the empty building the next day. He went on to say they had to be destroyed to prevent the new baby turkeys from catching some disease from them

I told him of my thoughts. He laughed and said fifty pounds was a lofty goal but maybe attainable if time wasn't a problem. He called me about three weeks later and said he had two that had escaped the catchers but one was larger than the other. I picked up the two white turkeys and brought them home. My wife seemed surprised at us having them until I told her of my plans. She turned and walked away shaking her head. I thought that was sort of odd. I mean everyone eats turkey at Thanksgiving and Christmas.

I put my turkeys of eight and twelve pounds in a pen and began to roll the feed to them. They really began to blossom. The weather began to cool down, so I went and talked to the father of our neighbor boy that grew up with our boys. He was a great neighbor and well versed in the old ways of doing things. I told him of what I had done and now it was time to think about processing the birds. George came over and looked at the turkeys and asked what I thought they would weigh.

I told him we would weigh them after we chopped their heads off. I told him if he would help kill and scald them, he could have one. He suggested chopping their heads off at our place then taking them up to his place to scald them. That way he could build a fire early in the morning and have time to get the water hot enough. He said it would be fun to process the birds like they did when he was just a boy. My plan was coming together.

Early December on a Friday I talked to him again and we made plans to process the birds the next morning. He came over just before ten and said it had taken that long to get the water hot enough. Now it was time. He asked how I planned on killing the turkeys. I showed him my big round piece of oak that we would put the turkey's head on.

"First we'll tie these heavy cords on the turkey's feet," I said. "Then after we chop off his head, we'll tie him up on that beam over the door of the pen to bleed out. Then we'll do the second one," I said proud of my plans. He said that sounded okay. I don't know why when things go wrong it seems I always have an audience. My wife was there, like always, trying to help where she could. We got the biggest turkey, laid his head on the oak stump and I did the honors. Together my neighbor and I tied the flapping crazed bird up over the doorway. He stayed up there for at least one half of a second before both cords broke and he fell into the dirt.

"Get him up, get him up, before he bruises himself all over," yelled George. We grabbed the flapping crazed thing and gave up trying to tie him up again. We just held him up off the ground until he quit flapping. "That went well," said George, grinning and listening to my wife's laughter.

"We'll use rope on the next one," I said.

"Good idea," said my neighbor.

We weighed the big one and he weighed forty-three pounds. The second one went a lot better with rope on his feet and only weighing thirty-nine pounds. Time to go scald the dead turkeys. We went up to George's house. He had a thirty-gallon metal drum setting on a grate over a fire with lots of red coals under it. He had a table of sorts, made from heavy 2x12's close to the drum.

"We'll pull his feathers out up there." he said.

Together we lifted the bird up high and into the almost boiling water. He began to slowly stir the bird around in the scalding water.

"We'll keep him in here for about two minutes then pull him up and try a feather. If it comes out easy, it's time to pluck him. If not, we stir him around some more," he said. Then he looked up and smiled. "It's going real good."

After a bit, he pulled the bird up again and tried a big wing feather. It pulled out easily.

"Time to get him out," he announced.

He grabbed one foot and I grabbed the other. The only problem was the feathers had absorbed some of the water and now the bird was almost the same size around as the thirty-gallon drum. He didn't come out.

"Pull, Paul. Pull!" yelled my neighbor. "If we don't get him out of there, we'll boil him with his feathers on."

We finally got him high enough straight up that we got him out of the scalding hot water. We got him up on the table and my neighbor turned into a turkey plucking machine. Feathers were flying in the air and all over. I jumped in and tried to give him a hand and together we got the feathers off the big bird. Only problem was he had been in the barrel too long and about half his skin had come off with the feathers. My wife was standing there laughing.

"Just look at you two," she said.

We looked at each other and laughed. We had feathers in our hair, all over our clothes. We were a mess. My wife came forward and looked at the bird.

"Boys," she said. "Now that is one ugly turkey."

We laughed and agreed and started on the next bird. It went a lot smoother being lighter and us being more experienced. My wife did her best on the ugly bird, but it was dry after being cooked. It didn't have enough skin left to hold the moisture in.

Since that day we have eaten many wonderful moist turkeys but none that we remember more than the one we worked on that day with our neighbor.

ALWAYS THINK BEFORE YOU ACT

S ometimes a simple task can go way wrong if we don't think before we act. I was sitting in our pickup while my wife was doing some shopping at a large store one warm fall day. I saw a large sign that read $3.95 in front of pumpkins stacked up in front of the store. Those were some big nice pumpkins for under four dollars, so I went over to take a better look. Man, they were great, so I decided to surprise her and have one waiting in the truck when she came out. They were stacked against the outside wall of the store four high. Naturally the bottom row was four wide, the next layer was three wide then two and then one row at the top.

They were all the same price and one was a lot bigger than the rest on the second row up from the bottom. It was almost perfectly round and would really be a good one to carve. It was stuck in there pretty good, but I kept working and with a final pull got it out. Then all heck broke loose. All those upper pumpkins began to roll down. Just a few at first and then it seemed that the whole pile was rolling down. They rolled down the pile. They rolled across the sidewalk. Then they started rolling off the sidewalk out into the parking lot.

I was doing my best to try to stop this avalanche of pumpkins, but it was like trying to stop 125 basketballs being rolled at you at the same time. I was really working at it and they were just starting to slow down when the store help came outside. I tried to apologize but they just started hauling pumpkins, so I went back and sat in the truck.

My wife came out a few minutes later and said, "Boy they sure have a mess over there." I started the truck and said, "Don't ask."

She giggled over half the way home then finally asked what happened. She still wishes she could have seen me in action that day.

A Broken Leg

—◦◦◦◦—

If the reader has never broken a bone as an adult it is an interesting event but not a lot of fun. I was opening our main gate behind our farmhouse one morning after we had another snow on top of the packed snow we already had. The packed snow had turned to ice in the tracks from our good old Dodge. Somehow one foot shot up in the air as my body twisted. I heard the bone break and felt that leg lose all strength and down I went. Lots of stuff went through my mind laying there. I kind of crawled and maneuvered over to the Dodge and pulled myself up and yelled towards the house. I don't know what she was doing but my wife couldn't hear me. I spotted the old shovel with the broken handle in the bed, so I pulled it out and started beating on the side of the Dodge.

Now it's not every day a farm wife looks up to see her husband beating his pickup with a shovel on a snowy day. She watched me for a minute and saw that I wasn't stopping so she came to the back porch. She yelled out, "Are you okay?"

"No," I yelled back.

Well here she came so I told her to go back in the house and get her coat. Like I said I had time to think several things over and was ready. "What's the matter?" she asked.

"I have broken my leg and I want you to listen to me," I said.

"What makes you think that your leg is broke?" she asked.

"I heard it and felt it give way, but I want you to listen to me," I said. She nodded her head okay. "I haven't fed or watered the cattle yet. They can go for a while without hay, but they have to have water. I want you to help me get into the truck, then you drive up and chop a hole in the ice then we will go to the hospital."

She leaned really close to my face and said, "You have lost your mind. We have to go to the hospital now."

I knew it was going to take some convincing to get her to understand. "Look, here's the deal," I said. "I can't let you go up there by yourself. If you slip and fall on this ice, I won't be able to help you, so let's just go up together, you chop a hole, then we can go to the hospital."

She really didn't like it one bit and I could see it all over her face. She was mumbling something about stubborn hard-headed men the whole time she helped me over to the passenger side and helped me get in. I didn't catch all of it. I gave her lots of advice up at the pond but she just gave me hard looks.

We knew the doctor that was on duty at the emergency room that day. We saw his feet walk up behind the curtain then he pulled the curtain back and yelled, "Cut it off at the knee," then pulled the curtain back closed. We all had a good laugh then he showed us the x-rays and yes, I had broken the small bone in my right leg. It took some time, but it healed up fine and all is good.

One thing, though. I'll never forget my wife leaning forward and telling me, "You have lost your mind."

JUST A LITTLE MORE

I believe most wives know that their husbands tend to go a little overboard when doing things. I don't know if it is genetics, hormonal or what, but we just need to turn it one more turn or get it a little tighter or just lift it a little higher. Most of the time that is when things really go south. We were not even thirty when we bought our small farm and the house wasn't much. There was a stack of quarter-inch wall paneling stacked in the corner of our bedroom left there by the previous owners. They had been bumped at one time and the top pieces had slid over sideways to make a long rectangular air space against the wall.

My wife had her sewing machine in that room sewing in front of the bedroom window. She began to tell me that wasps or hornets were bothering her. I was checking around and slid the top panel over and found the back side of a big gray hornet's nest next to the wall inside our bedroom. I went outside and found a small hole that had been used to run a telephone wire through and unfortunately hornets had found it also and were using it to go in and out of their nest.

I was going to take care of them, but it was going to take precise planning. I thought it over for at least three minutes and came up with my plan. It would involve a bath towel, a cotton ball and a can of bug spray. I need to stop here and make sure the reader learns that not all cans of bug spray are created equal. Really, some have much better knock down ability than others. Ant and roach spray works great on them, but not so much on hornets.

Proceeding with my plan I ever so gently pushed the bath towel in the back of the nest, blocking their escape into the bedroom, and went outside with my cotton ball. I waited until none were going in or out and stuck that cotton ball into the little hole. Now I had them where I wanted them. I went back in the house with my trusty can of ant and roach spray. I eased the bath towel away and sprayed them good then crammed the towel back in place. You could hear them in there. They sounded kind of like a chain saw running wide open under water.

They finally stopped making all that noise, so I knew I had nailed them good. I went outside and listened but couldn't hear anything. I began to wonder if that ant and roach spray had penetrated all the way to that side. I knew I would have to be quick but figured I should pull out the cotton ball and give them just a little more. I had my spray can right there to really give it to them, but I never got the chance. When I pulled out that cotton ball all heck broke loose. I was instantly on fire yelling and screaming and doing anything I could to get away from those hornets.

I ended up being stung seven times on my thumb and ten more times up my arm. I spent the rest of the day soaking my thumb in ice water. The next day we went to town and bought a can of hornet spray and finished them off.

You see the truth was they really did need just a little more.

A CITY COUSIN THAT FIT RIGHT IN

E very summer our boys had a cousin that would come and stay with us about a month. He and our boys would have a great time during his stay. My nephew liked slipping up on some big hogs we were feeding out and hopping on their backs for a short ride. A fat hog's back is really round so it was hard to stay on for very long, but he would hop on them and away they would go squealing for all they were worth and him laughing. It was getting close to the fourth of July and I had heard them talking of which fireworks stand had the best prices. My wife brought them home from town, and they were proud of their idea of pooling their money and getting a lot more stuff than last year. They had a large brown bag full of fireworks.

I went ahead with all my work and wasn't around them until the next evening. They were strangely kind of quiet. The next morning as I walked up to the main gate to the back pasture, I saw something big and black on the ground. I got up to the gate and started to smile. It was obvious why they had been quiet.

There were bits of charred brown paper bag all around the edges of a big burned out spot on the bare ground right by the gate. There were also little bottle rocket sticks all over. Their bag full of fireworks had somehow caught on fire and all went off at one time. Being farm kids they only sulked around for a day or so then found other ornery stuff to do.

Oh yes that city cousin is now a successful defense attorney, but I doubt if he rides hogs anymore.

BEING UPWARDLY MOBILE

O nce while working for an agricultural corporation it was time for our semiannual meeting. I knew that there was a mandatory human resource meeting scheduled. I don't know if the reader has been to many of these, but while they are necessary, most of them are dull and boring. Being upwardly mobile like I was I thought the best thing to do was buy a big pair of fake ugly teeth and bring a little joy to a few lives. I will have to be careful here because one person involved in this is still employed there.

I was seated next to a good friend of mine that worked out of the corporate office. About midway through the meeting I leaned over to him and asked if he was up for a little fun after the meeting. He answered with only one word, "Always." I slipped in my ugly fake teeth and smiled at him. With the smallest of smiles he nodded his head yes. The speaker was an up and coming woman in her early thirties and I have to say she gave a good presentation about all the changes coming up in our insurance program. Standing up after it was over, I said, "You be the straight man and just act dumb." My buddy slowly nodded yes.

There were a few people around the speaker asking questions, so we just stood there and waited our turn. When the last person had their question answered my buddy and I walked up, me with my head down. My buddy told her that I had a question and she turned to me. I looked up with those awful teeth in and asked, "How long do you have to work here before you can get on the dental program?"

Those teeth made it very difficult to speak and the words came out all slurred together. They were so big I couldn't completely cover them with my lips. Bless her heart she lowered her gaze to my new teeth and her eyes opened wide. Then being polite she looked over to my buddy's shoes then up to my forehead and began to ramble.

"I don't remember exactly, but I'm sure there is a waiting period. Yes, I'm sure there is a waiting period, but I can't remember how long it is."

Then she looked over to my buddy, called him by name and asked him if he knew how long it was. My buddy became instantly ignorant and slow of thought. He put the absolute dumbest look on his face and said, "I dunno."

Now everyone knew my buddy was well respected and had many articles published in trade magazines so I am sure she couldn't understand the sudden drop of his mental capabilities. So now she began to stammer even worse while making a circle with her vision of my forehead over to his face then down to his shoes across mine then up to my forehead.

I caught it just right and pulled out those ugly teeth. She made two or three more circles with her eyes then happened to look at my mouth. Those awful things were gone, and I was grinning at her.

She looked straight at my mouth then up to my eyes then jumped forward and grabbing me by my shoulders shook me a little. She started laughing uncontrollably and ran out of the room across the hall and into the woman's restroom.

The only thing was she still had her portable mike turned on and you could hear her laughing all around the hall. I told my buddy I don't know what she is going to do in there, but we had better have someone tell her the mike is still on. We got a female employee to go in and tell her.

All is well that ends well, but I still wonder where a guy with a P.H.D. ever learned to act that dumb and be the perfect straight man. As for myself, I always did try to be upwardly mobile.

ENJOYING LIFE IN THE WORKPLACE

I retired and took a job working part time at a warehouse so I could take advantage of their health insurance for my wife. Now days in the work place some things seem a little strange to me. Things like not letting part time employees clock in a few minutes early when they are there wanting to work. Then there are emails and mandatory company meetings. I was the lowest man on the totem pole so it didn't seem all that important to me to hear about corporate decisions. I mean, I was just unloading trucks and stocking shelves.

Well, we got word that we had to go to this company meeting over at the corporate office. I want to stop here and say I had a great supervisor and her boss was just great. These people ran a good warehouse and kept morale high. Six of us guys drove over there in two cars. We hadn't spent a lot of time there and had a little trouble finding the meeting room. We weren't late, just the last to arrive, so we stood against the wall by the door. It turned out to be a bio meeting. The man giving it was high up in HR and gave his bio that included a slide presentation and lasted over half an hour.

I thought I had been through some dry meetings but this one took the cake. I felt sorry for my boss's boss. She was on the front row dead center in front of the guy. When he finally finished, he asked how many there had never given a bio about themselves. About half of the people there raised their hands. Then they started telling of their work history and thankfully they kept theirs short. It was obvious that everyone was getting tired of this because the bios started getting even shorter.

Then it came to me that the way it was working out us guys against the wall would go last and I would be the first of our group. When my turn came, I stepped forward and with a good strong voice stated my name and that I worked in the warehouse with the rest of these distinguished looking gentlemen here against the wall and most of us are on work release programs from Federal Institutions. The room exploded with laughter, but I was watching my boss's boss. She kept her head down but slowly rotated it to the right where she could look at me. I just couldn't help it, I winked at her. Ever so slowly she shook her head then looked back down.

The good news is I kept that job until my wife got on Medicare and I resigned to do other things.

In closing all I can say is, I always kinda wanted to stand out in a crowd.

POOR FARM BOYS

A family moved in up the road from our farm when our sons were about eleven and thirteen. They had one son that was the same age as our youngest and soon he was over at our place doing stuff with our boys. If anything, he had less spending money than our boys. All summer long they would do stuff together always looking for something fun to get into. Our new neighbor boy turned out to be a great little mechanic. He fell into a good deal on a dirt bike in a box. That's right, he bought a motorcycle taken apart and put in a box.

He put it together and rode it up and down the dirt roads where we lived. It didn't take long until our youngest son bought it from him. All that morning the three of them rode it around the front pasture by our farmhouse. That wasn't daring enough so they built a small jump going away from the house. Since our youngest son was now the owner of the bike, he announced that he would go first. He got a good run and up and over the jump he went. When the motorcycle hit the ground, it flew into about fifteen pieces.

My wife and I were outside watching and heard our little neighbor say, "Oh no." He wanted to keep his money. He went running up there and all three began to pick up pieces. It took them several hours, but they put the bike back together and really tightened it down good and had it running before nightfall. The good thing was no one was mad or held a grudge. They were all used to making do with what they had. This was just another bump in the road to them. They stayed good friends and still are to this day.

FARM BOYS

We brought up our two sons telling them that they could do anything. They could be a doctor, lawyer, engineer, just anything they set their minds to. They retained the part about doing anything but not so much about the doctor-lawyer part. Growing up on the farm they did anything and everything that popped into their heads. When our oldest was about ten he decided to build a boat. After all it couldn't be that hard. Wood floats. He searched around and found some old boards and nailed them together in the shape of a large box. He did a pretty good job for his age, most of the seams only had a quarter-inch gap in them. When I mentioned the spaces in his boat, he proudly told me that it wouldn't make any difference because wood floats. He couldn't wait to try it, so I put his 'boat' into the back of our old Dodge and told his mother to get her camera.

I helped him get his 'boat' out of the truck at our

pond and got it over to the edge and gave him a little shove out into the water. We still have that picture of him paddling for all he was worth. He had that green pond water worked up into a good froth as his boat slowly sank. He came out of the pond with lots of that green scum on him and really perplexed. Any advice I had offered had been rejected so far, so I didn't offer any more at the time.

That small failure did not deter him from trying again because after all wood does float. He gathered up his younger brother and went out by the barn. I could hear them up there talking and hammering but I left them alone. A day and a half later they came and got me to come see what they had built. I walked all around the two wooden rafts they had built out of large wooden posts left over from farm projects. I told them I could only see one problem.

What? They wanted to know.

"How are you going to get them to the water? They will weigh over ninety pounds each."

"We really hadn't thought of that," they said.

I maneuvered them around and put one end in then slid the other end up into our pickup, then did it again and got the second one up in there. It looked like we were hauling long pieces of firewood.

I hauled them down to the swimming hole at the creek and drug out their rafts. Off they went happy as they could be. We ended up having to leave them down there because they were really dry and after absorbing some water they ended up almost doubling their weight. They were always doing things like that, always looking for new ways to have fun.

A little over a year later, on a beautiful spring day, I stepped outside in the afternoon and heard a bunch of yelling and screaming. I looked up and saw a sight I don't think I will ever forget. My oldest son was running the ridge line of one of our poultry houses while his younger brother was on the ground trying his best to knock him off by throwing big rocks at him. I went running right up there. Just as I got close the oldest yelled out, "Make him stop, Dad. He's going to kill me." I grabbed the younger one by the shoulder and spun him around to face me.

"What do you think you are doing?" I asked, almost yelling.

I want to say two things here. Never ask a question if you don't want to know the answer, and sometimes as parents we fail. With an open and honest face my youngest son said calmly, "Well, Dad, I'm trying to knock Travis off the roof with a rock."

He said it in a way like it should be very apparent to anyone. I can't tell you why but that hit me funny. I tried to turn quickly and not let the younger one see my face, and had to move away before I really began to laugh. Walking towards the house I yelled to the oldest, "Just do the best you can, son. You're on your own."

Well they both lived through it and the oldest escaped major injury that day. They both grew into adulthood without too many scars and now have teenage children of their own. Like I said early in this writing, I am now past seventy and have moved to town. Our oldest son now lives on the east coast but I guess he is still a farm boy at heart because one day the son of his younger brother came to me.

He asked, "Grampa, would you explain something to me about one of the old farm stories I have heard."

I told him I would if I could.

"I want to know why my dad was throwing rocks and trying to knock Uncle Travis off the roof of the chicken house when all he was doing was sitting up there reading the Bible."

I was shaking my head as I answered him. "I'm not real sure that is exactly the way that happened. You might want to ask your dad about that."

You see with farm boys the fun never stops.

ABOUT THE AUTHOR

In 1976 Paul bought a poultry farm in Southwest Missouri. Together, he and his wife raised their two sons there. They raised many different kinds of livestock on the farm.

He brings realistic humor and situations to his writings from the various people and experiences he has had along the way.

www.ingramcontent.com/pod-product-compliance
Lightning Source LLC
Chambersburg PA
CBHW071903020426
42331CB00010B/2654